His
Masterpiece

A Woman's Guide to Reclaiming Her Christian Identity

His

Masterpiece

A Woman's Guide to Reclaiming Her Christian Identity

Dominique Gardner

Copyright ©2017 by Dominique Gardner

Published by Extreme Overflow Publishing
A division of Extreme Overflow Enterprises, Inc
Grayson, Georgia 30017
www.extremeoverflow.com

Unless otherwise noted, all scriptures are taken from the
following versions of the bible: NLT, KJV, NIV, AMP, or ESV.

Manufactured in the United States of America
10 9 8 7 6 5 4 3 2 1

ISBN 978-0-6926546-8-2

TABLE OF CONTENTS

Purposeful Integrity
Sharing is Caring
The Invitation

Rewards on Earth
Rewards in Heaven

CLOSING PRAYER

ACKNOWLEDGEMENTS

To God, I give all the glory, honor, and praise!

To Isabella Rose.

There is a high price tag on your identity. May you always walk in this truth.

INTRODUCTION

Sitting at the table during freshman orientation, John walked into the room and my eyes lit up. I can remember saying to myself, "he's going to be my boyfriend." As I uttered these words I couldn't believe the boldness that came from my lips. You see, before John I never had a boyfriend. Nevertheless, freshman year of college was in full swing and within the weeks to come John and I were an item. People thought we were great together and even made cute nicknames for us. I couldn't believe it! I couldn't believe what I wanted actually happened! Unfortunately, the blissful feelings I had for John eventually faded. Soon enough, distrust and insecurity overwhelmed me. Ex-girlfriend drama was on the prowl and I found myself competing for the affection and the attention of a man I was immensely infatuated with. While my friends showed their love and concern by pointing out their unease for my relationship with John, I chose to continue believing that things would get better, and they did until Trisha came along.

Cornrows were a popular hairstyle at the beginning of the millennium. Of course Trisha was exceptional at braiding hair and John was sure to take advantage. Conveniently enough, Trisha would pick John up in her car and head to her house after hours so he could utilize her hair braiding services. He said they were "just friends," and I believed him. On many occasions, my friends tried to warn me not to be so naïve. But I wanted to believe that what I wanted, the desire I brought forth to reality, was indeed real.

Eventually, John broke up with me. He told me that he was not ready for a relationship. I was crushed. I remember wondering, was it because I wasn't enough? Was it my wardrobe? Was it my hair? Was it my figure? I can even remember pondering on ideas of how I could change his mind. No matter the conclusion I came up with, the end result was that John and I were not together.

In approaching sophomore year, all I could think about was how I would feel seeing John on campus, now as my ex-boyfriend. We spoke once over the summer, but I still envisioned what it would be like to see him face to face. My friend allowed me to drive her car back to campus and I was so anxious to see John I almost crashed her car!

The first day on campus I was sure to be intentional about how I looked. I wore high heels and a dress; two items I did not wear often. It wasn't long before I arrived on campus that I ran into John. That evening we strolled across campus talking and catching up. I told him how I had changed over the summer ensuring him that I was more grown up than the last time he encountered me. I even changed the way I walked to give the impression that I was more confident; holding my head up high while appearing more relaxed with every stride. Thinking about that time in my life now, makes me laugh because what I tried so hard to do really was silly. A woman never needs to convince a man of anything. When she knows she is a good thing, the right man will find her (Proverbs 18:22).

Eventually we started dating again and I became intentional about my appearance, as if changing my attire was going to fix everything wrong with our relationship. I also did my best to avoid John. I told people that I didn't want us to get bored with one another. The truth was that I didn't want him to lose interest in me again. I thought that if we spent more time away from each other, he would want me more. John's friends loved the idea and thought John had it made. My friends thought I had lost my mind. What mattered most to me was that John was happy and we seemed to be pretty happy as a couple. But just when it seemed like I had finally figured out how to keep this relationship working, things suddenly took a turn for the worst. By this time, it was summer. John only came to visit me once. He barely called and his disinterest seeped into our junior year.

Entering into our junior year, John was different. In came the influx of freshman and transfer students and out went our relationship. Women flocked to John and he loved it. In fact, I distinctly remember him saying that women were going to be attracted to him so, "just flaunt me," he would say. His statement left a bitter taste in my mouth. After disliking his reaction to the attention he was receiving, I couldn't take it anymore. The persistent flirtation with my roommate, other women, and undisclosed trips out of town to visit his "friend" Trisha, ripped my heart strings to pieces. And the hurt didn't stop there.

It wasn't long before I was being blamed for everything. John accused me of creating a fake social media account to not only harass Trisha but to also have my "ex-high school boyfriend" stalk her. John was the only boyfriend I ever had. Following his accusations arrived the onset of numerous text messages from an anonymous phone number with threats to come to my home and harm me because of my alleged behavior towards Trisha. When I explained to John that I was receiving threatening messages he didn't show any sense of concern. He told me that if it wasn't me that was causing all the havoc in Trisha's life, then I needed to find out who was. In my heart, I truly believed John and Trisha created this dramatic storyline, but I didn't have proof or understand the reason behind it.

Amidst all of the conflict and alleged allegations, my grades suffered greatly that year. I remember going to class or to work and not being able to hold myself together because all of the drama going on in my life. I can remember my supervisor, who could barely speak English, loving me enough to form the words to say she was concerned about me and her knowing the stress was directly related to the young man I was dating. Taking the role of mother away from home, she kindly let me know she did not approve of John. She was yet another person that observed his appalling character. I ended up on academic probation and was requested to write a letter stating why my grades plummeted and how I planned to get things back on track. Fortunately, the university gave me a second chance and I worked hard to try to get myself back on track.

Eventually my mother found out what was going on and called John's mother. After their discussion, John called me to apologize and began crying over the phone. I had never heard a man cry before and for some reason I had more compassion for him than myself **and the cycle continued;** John and I got back together. For a long period of time we did not have any issues. It was good, the way it was supposed to be. I was feeling more confident and showed it. I wasn't going to be made a fool, this time and I certainly did not want my heart broken, *again*. I made my presence known and began to assert my authority in the relationship. Eventually I ended up dominating the relationship and became almost like a mother figure to John, telling him what he could and could not do. That approach worked, until we graduated.

After graduation, something clicked for me. It was the first time I began to think about my future. It was the first time I had real responsibilities. I was no longer living in a bubble. With each passing year after college, I started to notice a change within myself. I realized that I was not that eighteen year old girl anymore and I wanted more out of life. I wanted more for myself and my relationship. As I began to think about what life would be like if I married John, I wondered what kind of husband or father he would be. Basing my chances of happiness on our relationship history, I knew a marriage between John and I just wouldn't last.

There was no better time to seek God than in that moment. I could feel him drawing me closer to him and the truth was, I needed him more than ever. As I began to draw nearer to Christ, my desires began to change and for the first time I saw Christ's reflection in me. To know Christ is to know his love. To know Christ is to know love's truest intentions (1st

Corinthians 13). The closer I drew to God, the more I realized that what I was missing out on was true love. It wasn't the need to know that I was beautiful, I knew that. I heard it all my life. What I needed to know was how much I was worth. I was worth so much more than the price tag I placed on myself. As I began to live my adult life outside of my inner circle, I began to see the world in an entirely different way. I began to see my worth.

In the years and months to come I learned that my value was priceless. Making the decision to accept this as my identity and walk confidently in this belief, would allow me to attract people who shared that same identity. I also learned that whether I allowed another man to enter into my life or not, *Jesus paid the price for me*, when he died on the cross and rose again, just for me. This alone makes me priceless! With my new "priceless" identity, I was able to start living my life as a woman who is whole and complete. And who did not have to lower her standards in any way to be happy in a relationship. I held a true understanding of Christ's priceless love which makes me elated to be the woman I am today.

In my last conversation to John, he expressed that if we were to get married, there would be a need for me to be the financial provider for our family, so that he could pursue his art career. That wasn't what God had in mind for me, his masterpiece. That wasn't God's divine will for my life. God had someone searching for a masterpiece of a woman. He already had someone for me wanting to match the love of Christ and enjoy God's magnificent work of art; his wife. God sent me a husband who said: "Yes she's absolutely worth that much!"

This is my story of how I took on the new identity of becoming God's masterpiece many years ago. While your story may be different, knowing your worth and understanding that you are God's masterpiece is unquestionably valid. In the chapters to come you will begin to uncover, explore and redefine the ways in which you view yourself, your life, and your purpose as God's masterpiece.

CHAPTER I

IDENTITY

Keep Your Chin Up, Grab Your High Heel Shoes & Walk with Strength & Dignity! (Proverbs 31:25)

Genesis 1:27 tells us that women were created in God's image. Being created in God's image exhorts our privilege to be a priceless masterpiece. So why then do so many women settle for a *worthless* identity instead of walking in the *worthy* identity of being liken to the image of God? To understand why, it is important to first understand the meaning of what identity is.

Identity is how you see yourself. In many cases identity is related to how you feel about the things you have no control over. For example, a woman can destroy her self-esteem by thinking she's *too short* or *too tall*. Some women destroy their self-esteem by thinking their hair is *too thick* or *too thin*. In other cases destroying your identity absolutely has to do with past experiences and hurts. This may include instances of being abused verbally, sexually, or mentally. It would even include being made fun of as a child or hearing your parents always compare you to your siblings or other people. Maybe everything you did in life didn't seem to be good enough for others. The fact is, you never know what makes a person walk with their head held low but know that giving value to these issues can cause you to adopt a worthless identity.

Something that is worthless has no value; it's insignificant. When you walk with a worthless identity, it can not only cause you to think less of yourself, it can also cause you to go far enough to think that you have nothing to offer anyone. Or even that you don't deserve anything good out of life. The harsh reality is that a woman who believes the lies of *worthless thinking* may also become a woman who has no or low standards. You see, a woman with low or no standards doesn't give into the plots, plans and tricks of the enemy because she wants to. Often times she may feel like she needs to do certain things for approval or love and so on. She may even carry a negative or manipulative attitude. You may know her as the woman who does whatever you tell her; she is a follower. You may even know this woman or be this woman. The reality of this woman boils down to the fact that this woman doesn't really know the depth of what God thinks about her. The truth is in God's word:

"We are God's masterpiece. He has created us anew in Christ Jesus, so we can do the good things he planned for us long ago."

Ephesians 2:10

A masterpiece is a great work of art. It's well thought out and put together perfectly. It doesn't have any imperfections. It's wonderfully made. That's what God thinks about us and that's how He made us. God's masterpiece resembles all of his creation, including you. This acknowledgement is easily blocked by low standards and the interpretation of life experiences. Or even by someone that showers you with things you want to hear, especially when they don't mean you any good. For example, think of a woman you know that may have never felt she was pretty enough. This woman will tread through life longing to hear someone say to them, "you're beautiful." And as soon as she hears it, she opens herself to even more and sometimes deeper hurt. Unfortunately, this is a dangerous place to be because it's so easy for a man that doesn't have good intentions to manipulate you, lure you into his bed, take your money, and have you paying his bills all because you needed his affirmation. Maybe that woman is you. Despite your past or your present, use today as a day to begin to walk with dignity knowing that you are God's masterpiece; fearfully and wonderfully made by Him (Psalm 139:14).

WOMAN OF DIGNITY

In the book of Proverbs we meet the virtuous woman. Proverbs chapter 31 verses ten through 31 provides great detail about her characteristics and lifestyle. In verse 25 we learn about her being a woman of strength and dignity.

When a woman walks in dignity she has self-worth, respect for herself and high self-esteem. The word "worth" generally means how much something cost or how valuable it is. When considering value we need to consider the cross.

For God made Christ, who never sinned, to be the offering for our sin, so that we could be made right with God through Christ.

2 Corinthians 5:21

Jesus thought you and I were valuable enough to have offered Himself up as a sacrifice for all our mistakes. He died for us to pardon of our sins and rose that we might be in right standing with God. This means that our mistakes and what people did or said about us can't keep us from our identity, dignity and power in Christ. Through salvation, all of the old stuff has passed away and *you have a new identity*. You are valuable!

The problem comes when we don't think of ourselves in that way. It is important to think of your worth as a "self-worth" concept not just "worth." So how valuable do *you* think you are? If you don't think you're worth anything great in life, great things will pass you by.

> *You are a chosen race, a royal priesthood, a holy nation, a people for his own possession, that you may proclaim the excellences of Him who called you out of the darkness into his marvelous light.*

> 1 Peter 2:9 ESV

Through his Word, God says that you are a "chosen race." This means that He selected you. You are a "royal priesthood." A woman that is royal is to be considered like a queen. A queen is someone people look to and respect. She shares wisdom and makes sensible decisions. She is a woman who walks with dignity. When she steps into a room she is noticed by her grace and poise. Her head is held high. After all, she's been crowned by a King and her crown lets society know who she is and what legacy she belongs to. In the same way, as we continue living for Christ we will receive the crown of life God has waiting for us when we meet him in heaven (James 1:12).

My dear, not only are you royal, you are a royal *priesthood*. This means that you have a job to do. Priesthood doesn't necessarily mean that you should jump up and pastor a church. It does mean that you have a job to do. God's kingdom needs you. Your life is a living witness of God's goodness that will draw others to want to be saved. As a royal priesthood, a queen in her own right, women can look to you and admire you because of the Jesus that emanates from inside of you. Think about your walk with Christ. Is your walk royal? Is it bringing others closer to Christ? The bible says, "Now you are the body of Christ and individually members of it (1 Corinthians 12:27)."

Each one of us has a role in serving the kingdom. It's up to all of us to represent Christ in the best possible way because we are His church.

But wait there's more! You are also a "holy nation" which means that even if you aren't living up to the standards that God has intended for you right now, God knows who He created you to be. You are better than whatever situation you may feel trapped in. You were designed to be the holy woman that God destined you to be. But first, what does it mean to be holy?

To be holy means to be sacred; set a part. Something that is sacred is preserved. It's purposely set apart from anything that is not like God.

> So put off your old self, which belongs to your former manner of life and is corrupting deceitful desires, and be renewed in the spirit of your minds, put on the new self, created after the likeness of God in true righteousness and holiness.

Ephesians 4:22-24

You are for "his own possession" which means that you are here to be in relationship with God. You are here for your life to glorify God in all that you do. You are not here to glorify anything or anyone else. You are a daughter of the most-high king. You are a child of God. You are here to reverence Him and Him only. If we live our lives right in the sight of God we will be received back to Him to live forever with Him in heaven. The Word says, "I will make you my wife forever, showing you righteousness and justice, unfailing love and compassion (Hosea 2:19)." In the same way God is like the husband and we the church are His wife. In marriage the husband clings to his wife and the wife clings to her husband. They leave their parents and families to create a covenant between each other that no one can separate.

A man leaves his father and mother and is
joined to his wife, and the two are united into
one. This is a great mystery, but it is an

illustration of the way Christ and the church

are one.

Ephesians 5:31

Therefore, we do not belong to our mother, father, children, husband, or boyfriend. We belong to God and we'll be given back to God. "Once you had no identity as a people; now you are God's people. Once you received no mercy; now you have received God's mercy (1 Peter 2:10 NLT)." This is all because of the love of Jesus Christ and because of the love of Jesus Christ, we know who we are.

You are exactly what God says you are in His word! "You are more precious than jewels *and* your value is far above rubies *or* pearls (Proverbs 31:10).

WOMAN OF STRENGTH

As a woman of worth, dignity, who is fulfilling a royal priesthood as a holy nation for his possession, you are also full of strength and power. Someone who has strength and power tries her best not to walk in fear. Instead she walks with the mindset that she has God with her wherever she goes. She sings,

The Lord is my strength and shield. I trust him with all my heart. He helps me, and my heart is filled with joy. I burst out in songs of thanksgiving!

Psalm 28:7

She knows that her strength doesn't come from her alone. She is not arrogant to think that she can handle life's challenges on her own. She knows her strength is not physical but is spiritual coming from the Holy Spirit.

While the Holy Spirit is inside of her she is strong and she has the power to overcome any weakness she may have. With Christ, she has the power to overcome the devil and his tactics.

My grace is sufficient for you, for my power is made perfect in weakness. Therefore I will

boast all the more gladly of my weaknesses, so that the power of Christ may rest upon me. For the sake of Christ, then, I am content with weaknesses, insults, hardships, persecutions, and calamities. For when I am weak, then I am strong.

2 Corinthians 12:9-10

Leaning on God's word empowers you to lay your burdens down when life is difficult to handle. Whether it is now or sometime in the future, you may deal with a situation that makes you feel like you can't go on. At one time or another you may have had people say you weren't smart enough, pretty enough, educated enough, or tough enough. Maybe you don't know how you're going to make ends meet. Or maybe you're trying to get out of a negative relationship. Maybe you didn't have a mother or father around to pour into you and raise you and it left you fending for yourself all your life. Know that

God is your strength and when you feel weak you can ask God to help you; that is your strength!

In Proverbs 31, the bible says that the woman was "clothed in strength and dignity and she laughed without fear of the future (Proverbs 31:25)." This means two things:

1. **Strength & Dignity has a look.** In contrast to being unclothed, to be *clothed* means that you wear it, you're covered. It means her esteem and dignity is covered by knowing where her strength comes from. It comes from God. Most of the time, people think about designers and how a piece of clothing is going *to* fit them. The Proverbs 31 woman wears the ultimate designer apparel. The Proverbs 31 woman's designer is God! Therefore, she has no need in finding the right size because strength and dignity are always her perfect fit. When you walk in these designer threads, others will want to wear them too. Knowing who you are and holding your head up high looks good on you. So that makes

you a trendsetter. Other women will want to know what's so different about you! What they'll find out is that you're wearing your identity! What they'll find, is that you know who you are and whose you are. With your designer attire, you'll be the one to lead someone else to Christ.

2. **A Woman with Strength & Dignity lives fearlessly.** This woman laughs without fear. She isn't afraid of what's to come. She gives her worry and stress to God. She is full of life, joy, and peace. A woman that is fearless is rare. The only way that anyone can truly live a fearless life is by standing on God's Word. God's Word keeps us mentally and emotionally stable. It builds our faith. It's time to place that crown on your head, lift your chin up, put your high heels on, and start walking royally. You're a daughter of the King and you've got places to go! It's time to walk "out of the darkness into his marvelous light!" (1 Peter 2:9)

If you feel like you're a woman living each day with a "worthless" identity it's time to make a change. One of the best ways to understand your worth is to see yourself how God sees you. The only way to know how God sees you is by reading his word. Your identity can always be found in him. Start wearing you're crown this week and for the rest of your life. Every time you look in the mirror repeat these words: "I am God's masterpiece!"

CHAPTER 2

REJECTION

Stand Strong, Stand Firm, You are a Living Stone.

(1 Peter 2:4-6 ESV)

Not accepting the identity God has given you can stem from insecurity. Sometimes insecurity stems from rejection. You can be rejected socially which is when people exclude themselves from anything that deals with you. You can also reject yourself. When you have rejected yourself, typically what you've done is believe your identity or value is the opposite of what God created you to be. For example, you can reject yourself because you believed what someone did to you or the horrible things they told you about yourself; that aren't true. You can also reject who God wants you to be because sometimes change can seem too hard.

With any way it is presented, rejection hurts. This hurt reflects how we see ourselves through the perspective of others. Although rejection is certainly difficult to deal with, you must give all of the pain that comes from rejection to God. These hurts can no longer dominate your life. You're not alone. If anyone understands, God certainly does.

A woman who rejects herself does so because she is insecure. Society tells women that they have to be a certain height, weight, or have a certain skin tone in order to be accepted. Sometimes women feel like they're too light or too dark. Some feel like they're too young to do anything of value while others feel like time has run out and they're just too old. And of course there's our figure. Some may feel like they need to lose a few pounds and for others it's just the opposite. Media tells us that we should drink, smoke, have sex on a whim with multiple partners, and of course party all the time! Society tells us that it's about us and not about God and furthermore there is no God. Society tells us that we should follow the trends, even as the trends change each season. This can feel like your uniqueness is suffocating forcing you to be someone else rather than your true self.

Looking at a different version of 1 Peter 2:9 uses an interesting spin on the next point.

*"But ye are a chosen generation, a royal priesthood, a holy nation, **a peculiar people**; that ye should shew forth the praises of him who hath called you out of darkness into his marvelous light.*

1 Peter 2:9

To be peculiar means that you are different. You stand out. You don't follow the trend and therefore you most certainly do not follow the world.

When you walk in your new identity people might not agree that you're qualified or capable to do the things you're gifted to do and that's ok. God has already approved you. However, if you follow the world's standard you'll reject yourself; God's divine will for your life. You'll look at yourself and think you need to be someone else to do anything great in life. You'll think you need to have the right degree and/or pedigree before you become a woman of value. None of which is true. God is so awesome in that sometimes he will raise up the most unlikely candidate to do extraordinary things. In this way God is glorified and you will realize you're perfect just the way you are. If God didn't create you specifically the way you are (and with what you think you don't have or what you want to get rid of), you wouldn't be able to accomplish what He has called you to do!

The Most Unlikely Candidate

Within the book of Genesis 27 we meet twin brothers; Jacob and Esau. Esau is the older brother and Jacob the younger. From society's standard, the first born son should receive the birthright which is a double portion of his father's inheritance and a special blessing. In this case the younger brother

Jacob received not only the inheritance but the blessing as well (Genesis 27: 28-29). This was the blessing found in Genesis 27 where God told Abraham "serve you, and nations bow down to you (Genesis 27:29)." God didn't go by society's standard but his sovereign standard showing us that He establishes what is right. God establishes the standard. The bible tells us that Esau was ungodly which is why God could not use Esau to be in the line of the Abrahamic covenant (Hebrews 12:6). God needed to use someone who loved Him to represent the people He loved, the Israelites.

Further into Genesis 37 we meet a young man by the name of Joseph along with his brothers. Joseph was second to the youngest of his brothers and his father was always giving him special treatment. The kind of treatment you would expect the firstborn son to receive. Sound familiar? Joseph also had a special gift that no one else had. He was a dreamer. God would speak to him through dreams and He would tell Joseph the things to come. Interestingly enough,

He told Joseph that one day he would rule over his brothers. Well when Joseph told his brothers they didn't like it. In fact, in Genesis 37:27 his brothers got so angry they sold him into slavery. Even though he had some setbacks, God still raised Joseph up to rule not only over his brothers but an entire nation of people.

And Moses, he was a man of great fear and little faith. In Exodus chapter 3 God called Moses to lead His people; the Israelites, out of slavery and into the land of Canaan, the promised land. While God called Moses, Moses continued to respond through his feelings instead of having enough faith in God to step up and lead his people. Chapter 3 illustrates a good picture of how Moses felt about himself. He didn't consider himself a leader. He didn't consider himself a great speaker due to his stuttering problem and to top it off he was afraid to speak to Pharaoh, the "brother" he grew up with. In chapter 3 Moses goes back and forth with God countless times until God allows Moses' brother Aaron to go with Moses and speak for him.

In becoming God's masterpiece, it is important to recognize the power of God moving in our lives whether we are qualified or not. When God calls you to a task he is working through you. So it doesn't matter if you think you are not qualified. What matters is that you understand that God loves you, thinks you're special and He is the one who qualified you. Wherever you feel you fall short, He is strong (2 Corinthians 12:9-11).

God doesn't make mistakes He makes masterpieces! He's made you alternate to society's current trend and standard so He can be glorified through your life. At the same time, God isn't looking for a person that the world would naturally showcase. He's looking for the person with a heart for Him. Only then can He make you into a wonderful accomplishment and victory. If you don't love the person He created you to be then it will be hard for you to not only accept your rightful identity but also your God-given purpose. There are people waiting on you to take your place and most certainly encourage other women to become masterpieces!

The story of Saul and David provides a great illustration of a person who does not fit society's standard of a capable leader but God says otherwise. Saul was naturally better suited to be king from his outward appearance of being tall, handsome, and fit. Unfortunately, Saul had a problem with taking directions from God as he led his people which resulted in the search for a new king.

> *The Lord has torn the kingdom of Israel from*
> *you today and has given it to someone else—*
> *one who is better than you. And he who is the*
> *Glory of Israel will not lie, nor will he change*
> *his mind, for he is not human that he should*
> *change his mind!*

1 Samuel 15:28-28

Saul's time was up due to an identity crisis so God commanded Samuel to anoint a new king. The Lord sent the prophet Samuel to Jesse the Bethlemite to search for the new king saying, "For I have provided myself a king among his sons (1 Samuel 16:1)." Immediately, Samuel looked at the outward appearance of Jesse's son Eliab and made the assumption that he was the one God wanted to anoint. However, the Lord spoke to Samuel and said,

Don't judge by his appearance or height, for I have rejected him. The Lord doesn't see things the way you see them. People judge by outward appearance, but the Lord looks at the heart.

1 Samuel 16:7

God is looking at the heart not your outward appearance. Outward appearance will not show you if a person will be obedient to God. Outward appearance will not show you if a person is right for the job, no. Being used by God is all about a person's being heart fixed towards Him. So Samuel called each

41

of Jesse's sons until he got to the sixth one and he still felt that he hadn't come in contact with who the Lord had chosen.

> *Samuel said to Jesse, "Are these all the sons you have?" "There is still the youngest," Jesse answered. "He is tending the sheep." Samuel said, "Send for him; we will not sit down until he arrives." "Rise and anoint him; this is the one." So Samuel took the horn of oil and anointed him in the presence of his brothers, and from that day on the Spirit of the Lord came powerfully upon David."*

1 Samuel 16:11-13

Isn't it interesting that out of all Jesse's sons, God chose the son that was out tending the sheep? God's ways are not our ways. He does not think like us. He is all knowing and all powerful.Therefore, God did not choose David by outward appearance. God chose someone who had a heart for him.

The spirit of the Lord was upon David. But an evil spirit was upon Saul; due to his pride and disobedience. So when Saul's servants brought in David to play the harp for him so that Saul could be well they talked about David, and described him by saying,

*"Behold, I have seen a son of Jesse the Bethlehemite, who is skillful in playing, a man of **valor**, a man of war, prudent in speech, and a man of good presence, and the Lord is with him."*

1 Samuel 16:18

Wow! What great attributes David had! As a result, of David's description, David was placed in Saul's service and became his armor-bearer. David continued his duties tending his father's sheep and playing music for Saul. And when the people of God were challenged by Goliath the champion of the Philistines, he didn't fall back like everyone else did, he rose to the occasion. Now, as great of a man as

David was, no one had any faith in him. Because of his physical appearance no one even thought that he could help fight a battle, let alone win. "Don't be ridiculous!" Saul replied. "There's no way you can fight this Philistine and possibly win! You're only a boy, and he's been a man of war since his youth (1 Samuel 17:33 NLT).

But David was unstoppable. David did not let the reservations of what other people thought of him stop him from conquering a giant. He replied to their disbelief with confidence and strength because he knew the Lord was with him. So, David said to Saul,

"Your servant used to keep sheep for his father.
And when there came a lion, or a bear, and took
a lamb from the flock, I went after him and
struck him and delivered it out of his mouth.
And if he arose against me, I caught him by his
beard and struck him and killed him. Your
servant has struck down both lions and bears,
and this uncircumcised Philistine shall be like

one of them, for he has defied the armies of the

living God." And David said, "The Lord who

delivered me from the paw of the lion and from

the paw of the bear will deliver me from the

hand of this Philistine." And Saul said to

David, "Go, and the Lord be with you!"

1 Samuel 17:34-37

Even as David went in to battle with Goliath, Goliath also challenged him on his physical appearance. Yet again, David did not let the words of the world stop him but instead walked in his identity in Christ knowing his purpose to fight for victory. David said to Goliath,

"You come to me with a sword and with a spear

and with a javelin, but I come to you in the

name of the Lord of hosts, the God of the armies

of Israel, whom you have defied. This day the

Lord will deliver you into my hand, and I will

strike you down and cut off your head. And I

will give the dead bodies of the host of the

Philistines this day to the birds of the air and to the wild beasts of the earth that all the earth may know that there is a God in Israel, and that all this assembly may know that the Lord saves not with sword and spear. For the battle is the Lord's, and he will give you into our hand."

1 Samuel 17:45-47

After this, David defeated Goliath and the Philistines fled. After all that people said that David couldn't do, God used him, the most unlikely candidate to rise to victory.

Have people counted you out when you know that God has designed you for so much more? You are not alone. God has not forgotten about you. He loves you! What others think about you is not the measurement that determines your capabilities. Limiting yourself to the standards of what others think you're capable of doing will only leave you accomplishing much less than what you know God has gifted you to do. You're not always going to have people rooting for you. In fact, when you make a mistake it is common for others to recall your error before they remember any impact you've ever made. Here is the deal, this Christ walk is not about being perfect. It is about knowing who you are in Christ and trying to live what Christ commands of you. As for King David, the least likely candidate by society's standards; he won victory, after victory, after victory. So can you!

When you think about Christ, you may think about the king of kings and Lord of lords. He is the son of God. He is full of power and might. Alongside people everywhere angels worship Him. He's our healer, protector, and provider. But even Christ was viewed as the least likely candidate.

In today's terms, Christ was born on the "wrong side of the tracks." A manger isn't a place a king is born, however, God orchestrated things that way to make a bold statement. God seeks to exalt the lowly things of the world to work out His plans here on

Earth. We find this in Mary's song when she says "He has brought down the mighty from their thrones and exalted those of humble estate (Luke 1:52)." From the world's standard, Jesus was not what they considered a king but God chose him the same way he chose you.

REJECTION AND PAST MISTAKES

What if a past mistake is keeping you bound and feeling rejected. In the book of Luke chapter 7, there was a woman who heard that Jesus was in town. She grabbed an alabaster box full of perfume and went to him. "And standing behind Him at His feet, weeping, she began to wet his feet with her tears and wiped them with the hair on her head, kissed his feet and anointed them with the ointment (Luke 7:38)." Society had rejected this woman, but her courageous display of reverence to Christ is what caused her sins to be forgiven.

No matter how you may feel about yourself because of your past and no matter what others have said about you, once you truly seek Christ's forgiveness you have it. Another example of God's love and forgiveness is through the story of Saul of Tarsus. Saul was a very privileged, educated, and prideful man. In describing himself he stated,

> *I was circumcised when I was eight days old. I am a pure-blooded citizen of Israel and a member of the tribe of Benjamin – a real Hebrew if there ever was one! I was a member of the Pharisees, who demand the strictest obedience to the Jewish law. I was so zealous that I harshly persecuted the church. And as for righteousness, I obeyed the law without fault.*

Philippians 3: 5-6

Boy was this guy feeling himself. He thought he was perfect.He thought believing in God meant being obedient to the Jewish law, in which he found no fault in himself. As a result he saw fit to persecute anyone that believed in Christ. Countless Christians were martyred at the account of Saul. So naturally, you wouldn't think that Saul would be someone that God would use. But He did. On Saul's way to Damascus, while he was in pursuit of more Christians to murder, he had an encounter with God that changed his life forever. On the road to Damascus, God blinded Saul and demanded that he explain his wicked behavior. For three days Saul was blind; until the disciple Ananias came to heal him.

And immediately something like scales fell from his eyes, and he regained his sight. Then he rose and was baptized; and taking food, he was strengthened.

Acts 9:18

After Saul's encounter, he changed his name to Paul. This is the account of Saul's new identity. He became an apostle starting churches, preaching the gospel, and leading others to Christ. He even went on to write a large portion of the New Testament contributing 13 books. Through the story of Paul's conversion, we can see that someone as prideful as Saul can be redeemed by God and used for His glory. In this way, no one can boast about being perfect in any area.

Society may tell you that there is an error in the way God designed you. "For we are God's masterpiece. He has created us anew in Christ Jesus so we can do the good things He planned for us long ago (Ephesians 2:10)." No matter what, the world isn't going to change its ways. You have to walk in the wisdom to know that while society may tell you lies about your physical identity, you are beautiful in both your physical and spiritual identity. As the scripture says, "If the world hates you remember it hated me first (John 15:18)." Without a doubt, you have to be strong and know who you are. You are a daughter of the King!

———————

This week set your prayers to ask God to help you to see all the areas you've felt rejected. Through prayer, meditation, and with time allow Him to remove the rejection from your heart. Let God heal you. Pray also that God shows you who you really are with all the gifts and talents He has placed inside you. Even ask Him about your purpose in life. Remember God doesn't make mistakes, He makes masterpieces!

CHAPTER 3

STAYING FOCUSED

O God, you are my God; earnestly I seek you; my soul thirsts for you; my flesh faints for you, as in a dry and weary land where there is no water. (Psalm 63:1 ESV)

It's one thing to acknowledge areas for growth but, how do you keep yourself on the right track? How can you make sure you're growing in Christ and not allowing the enemy to keep you defeated? How can you make sure you are spiritually healthy and whole? How can you make certain that you are becoming the woman God intended you to be? The simplest answer is, through relationship. You need to make sure your relationship with Christ is authentic and that you are intentional about seeking Him. Well, what does all that mean?

RELATIONSHIP

When you think about the word relationship you would most likely think about the connection between two individuals. There's something that draws them to one another. There's something they have in common and you could also suggest there's something they need from one another. Considering the relationship of a father and his daughter, what do you think connects them? For the daughter she probably looks at daddy as her provider. When she looks up at him she probably sees him as the strongest person she knows.

For a father, his daughter is the apple of her eye. He wants her to take care of herself by eating all her vegetables, doing well in school, and of course being obedient. Their relationship has a strong foundation due to the quality time they spend with one another.

When she has questions, she asks him and he advises her. When she's afraid of the monsters under the bed, he's there to protect her and to let her know everything' will be alright. He's her hero.

This father daughter relationship mirrors the intended relationship between a woman and her Heavenly Father. Our father wants us to live out our purpose and rely on Him. In the same way that we need our father in every area of our lives, we need his guidance, his provision, and his love. A relationship requires the effort of both individuals. God is always present. The problem is when we are quick to become disconnected and disheveled when really we haven't done our part.

All we have to do is seek Him daily. He tells us, "You will seek me and find me, when you seek me with all your heart (Jeremiah 29:13)." These words from the Lord came from a letter written by the prophet Jeremiah. He was giving the Israelites a message from God. God's people the Israelites were in exile for 70 years when they should have been free the entire time. Because they chose not to seek the Lord with their whole heart they were stuck in a dry land because they made the choice to have their focus on everything outside of Christ. All God wanted was a true authentic relationship with His chosen people in exchange for all the blessings He had in store for them.

If you want true peace and abundance in your life you have to have an authentic relationship with Christ. That means that you are consistent in your walk. God wants to be your strength. God wants you to know what you're worth. God wants you to see yourself the way He sees you. God wants you to give all your burdens to Him. It starts with Him.

THIRSTING FOR HIS PRESENCE

Have you heard the story of Mary and Martha? Well, Mary and Martha were sisters and at the sight of Jesus coming into town Martha invited Him into her house. Immediately Martha was preoccupied with serving and making sure everything was perfect. Her sister Mary, sat at Jesus' feet. At the sight of not receiving help she had a bit of an emotional breakdown and tried to make her sister look as if she wasn't being helpful. It would have seemed as if Mary was being lazy until Jesus replied,

"Martha, Martha, you are anxious and troubled about many things, but one thing is necessary. Mary has chosen the good portion, which will not be taken away from her."

Luke 10:41-42

This is a great illustration of what God really wants; time and attention. Jesus didn't care about these two ladies trying to be perfect. Nor was he concerned with who was serving Him the best meal. He was impressed by the woman with a heart for him. He was impressed by the woman who wanted to learn everything He had to share. He was impressed by the woman who wanted to obtain everything He had to offer.

The story of Mary and Martha also illustrates Mary's thirst for God. Most women have experienced a time of spiritual instability where superficial things once meant everything, but when you get to a place of wholeness nothing else satisfies you the way Christ does. Romance, the idea of getting married, your career, and even material possessions can consume you when Christ isn't number one. However, when you get to the point of desiring a true authentic relationship with Christ, your relationship with him is all that matters.

When you have a thirst for God you not only seek Him through His word, but also through prayer time. Every woman needs that quiet secret place where she can go and sit at Jesus' feet just like Mary. This is the place where you can lay your burdens down. This is the place where you can cry out to God and learn what it truly means to place your trust in Him. This is a place where you can make your petitions known. This is a place where you can dwell in his presence and commune with Him. When you get to this point in your relationship with Christ, you realize that running to Christ should be your first priority rather than running to human beings about what concerns you.

A woman that is whole and complete doesn't lean on the guy she's dating to solve her problems. She goes to the Lord. A woman of wholeness doesn't worship the ground her boyfriend walks on, she worships Christ. A woman that is complete because of Christ doesn't call every person in her cell phone to get advice on a particular situation. She gets in God's face and heeds His direction. So I ask you, how thirsty are you for his presence?

When you're in the presence of God your entire countenance will change as well. You'll have a glow. I've noticed this to be true about myself. In my life I have noticed the times where I am out of balance with my relationship with Christ because you can see it on my face. When I'm focused on issues or problems instead of seeking Christ it shows outwardly. I look extremely exhausted, bothered, and unhappy. I'm not as social and usually very tense. However, the times when I am seeking the Lord constantly, I have a glow. I'm bubbly, vibrant, peaceful, and I generally have a softer countenance. Believe it or not, this causes me to feel more lady-like and less rigid. It also causes me to feel more confident because I know that I am in right standing with God.

This feeling is very much like I would imagine the feeling Moses had at Mount Sinai. After speaking with the Lord, Moses' face glowed:

> *When Moses came down from Mount Sinai carrying the two Tablets of The Testimony, he didn't know that the skin of his face glowed because he had been speaking with God. Aaron and all the Israelites saw Moses and saw his radiant face.*

Exodus 34:29-30

This kind of glow replaces everything Maybelline, Sephora, and Mac can do all together. This is the type of glow to strive for as Christian women!

THIRSTING FOR HIS WORD

Standing on the word of God is helpful to your life as a believer. The word of God is designed to encourage you to hear God's voice and direction when you're lost and to give you discernment so you won't be lead astray by those that misuse the Word. When you're down and not feeling your best, meditating on the Word of God can lift your spirit. Early in my walk I would always carry around Joyce Meyer's book, *"The Secret Power of Speaking God's Word."* It's a book that you can keep in your purse and it has tons of scriptures that range from topics like depression, loneliness, finances, anxiety and so much more. Meditating of the Word of God keeps you focused instead of allowing the enemy to trap you into becoming defeated. No matter if you're just starting your walk with Christ or if you're seasoned, depending on the circumstance your faith may waver because you're focused on the issue instead of the solution being Christ. We should always remember the power in meditating on God's word to keep us lifted.

One of the areas that I continually struggled with in my 20's was the ability to hear God's voice. I would pray but I didn't realize just how much the word of God was needed for me to understand what God was saying to me. There are so many stories in the bible that directly relate to what we are dealing with in the present day. Even though the bible was written long ago, it was written with all of us in mind. It helps us to understand who God is and who we are in Him. There have been several times when a woman has come to me when she is trying to discern whether the person she is dating is "the one" God has sent to be her husband. I always tell women to go to the Word of God because the bible clearly tells us the characteristics of a mate.

Maybe it's the job offer you just received or maybe you're wondering if you should go back to school. Even in the area of finances, I continually ask the Lord to give me wisdom in how much I should spend and save. A woman with a heart for God is going to continually seek Him to direct her path in every area of her life. Psalm 119:105 says, "Your word is a lamp to my feet and a light to my path." This means that she doesn't walk through life haphazardly. In the same way, a master piece isn't completed haphazardly. Every step we take should be governed by the Holy Spirit.

The word of God also imparts in us the gift of discernment. Now discernment is certainly a gift you can and should pray for. However, having a deep understanding of the word of God can truly enhance this spiritual gift. Discernment allows you to see things that aren't right about situations and people in an effort to protect you. Let's look at the story of Jesus when He was tempted by Satan in the wilderness.

Jesus had been fasting for forty days and forty nights when Satan came on the scene to tempt Him with food. Satan even tried to twist scripture to fool Jesus into falling into his trap. Jesus knew the word of God very well so He couldn't be fooled. He replied, "Man shall not live on bread alone, but every word that comes out of the mouth of God." Matthew 4:4. The bible is our nourishment. When we are weak relying on God makes us strong so we can stay on track. Every time the devil tried to tempt and fool Jesus, He fired back with scripture.

We all have and will be tempted by Satan whether he works through people or pushes a nerve in areas where we are weak. We have to remember God is our strength. His word keeps us stable so we don't stumble.

The temptations in your life are no different
from what others experience. And God is
faithful. He will not allow the temptation to be
more than you can stand. When you are
tempted, he will show you a way out so that
you can endure.

1 Corinthians 10:13

The way out, is his Word. So when someone comes to you and tells you that you're not good enough, you'll remember Zechariah 2:8 which says, "Anyone who harms you harms my most precious possession!" When someone tries to tempt you into doing something dishonest or even when someone tries to twist scripture in an effort to make sin acceptable, you won't fall. You'll stay on track because you know what the Word of God says. There have been many times in my life where I've felt that people haven't had my best interest in mind. I've also felt times where scripture had been twisted for manipulation. If you end up in a situation that seems a little shady, because of your relationship with Christ, your knowledge of the Word of God, and a discerning spirit, you'll know when it's time to leave. Stay focused.

This week spend some time with Jesus. You can keep it simple and just have a quick chat. Maybe next week you can chat but this week spend some time in silence and then listen to what He wants to say to you. If there are particular areas where you need to hear God's voice, pull out your bible as another tool for clarity. Just like learning a new instrument or learning how to ride a bike keep trying and continue to make progress. Don't worry about if you fall. Just like you normally would. Dust yourself off and keep going. You're a masterpiece in the making!

CHAPTER 4

THE BEAUTY OF BRAINS

Charm is deceptive, and beauty is fleeting;

but a woman who fears the Lord is to be praised.

(Proverbs 31:30 ESV)

Making a commitment to the Lord is a lifestyle change. Once you're truly committed, not only does your countenance change, but everything that is not of God just won't be desirable anymore. What the world has to offer won't satisfy you. I can truly say that over the years the more time I spent with Christ the more my desires changed. The music I listen to now and the friendships I have today are completely different from when I first became a Christian. There are several types of movies and television shows that

I choose not to watch because of how it can affect my spirit or because of the negativity it promotes.

When you're whole and complete, any idol you've placed before the Lord, won't even be a thought. You'll represent, Romans 12:1(NLT) which says, "And so, dear Christian friends, I plead with you to give your bodies to God. Let them be a living and holy sacrifice-the kind he will accept. "When you're committed to living a life for Christ, you are holding yourself to a higher standard than before and you'll be mindful that everything you do and say should be for the glory of God.

As women, one of the areas that we struggle with the most is our conversation. It's easy to communicate out of our emotions instead of letting the Holy Spirt lead us in the words that we say.

When you're in the fullness of your relationship with Christ the Holy Spirit will convict you and you will desire His conviction. You will walk with poise, confidence, and everything you say will be seasoned with salt (Matthew 5:13). Other women will gravitate to the Holy Spirt that is inside of you and they will want to be around you. We referenced Proverbs 31 in chapter 1 but let's take another look. There are a couple of passages that we can analyze. Proverbs 31:26 says, "She opens her mouth with wisdom, and the teaching of kindness is on her tongue." A woman of wholeness thinks about what she says before she says it.

A lot of times people wonder why I don't speak often during conversations. There have been so many times when people think I am not interested in group discussions or that I have nothing of value to offer in the conversation. In my opinion sometimes people really like to hear the sound of their own voice. When I'm in a conversation with another person a lot of times I sit back and listen. I want to make sure that I give a thoughtful response because words matter and words certainly have power. Giving a thoughtful response and the tongue being seasoned with salt means your response will be given to you by the Holy Spirit.

In a society driven by "mean girls," the woman who fears God will appear to be the exact opposite. Not only does she think before she speaks, but her words are kind and uplifting. Many women have grown up to not trust one another and a lot of times when a woman walks in the room she's checked up and down by other women who are judging whether or not they see her as competition.

A woman that fears God knows who she is and doesn't have time for pettiness. A woman who is whole and complete can easily walk up to another woman and say, "Wow! I love your shoes!" She can compliment an entire outfit because she knows who she is and she knows her sister in Christ is valuable also. A kind and thoughtful word goes a long way and people will remember you for it (Psalm 15:1).

A woman of wholeness isn't seeking to be loved because she knows that Christ gave the ultimate sacrifice for her. Therefore, she knows just how much she is loved. She also knows that she is called to return that same love to others. Proverbs 31:20 says, "She opens her hand to the poor and reaches out her hands to the needy." You are called to love and to serve also, girlfriend!

There are so many ways that you can you can show love and serve. Now like the scripture says you can certainly have a heart for those in need. You can give to those who are less fortunate. You can pay if forward and pay for the person behind you in the drive-thru at Starbucks. You can even pay for someone's groceries. You can also simply ask someone how you can be praying for them during the week. There is so much beauty in giving.

A woman who fears the Lord allows the Holy Spirt to take residence in her heart and she becomes more and more like Christ every day. She's whole from the inside out so she's not looking to get anything from others. Instead she's searching for ways to help the body of Christ grow and maintain a healthy state. A woman who fears the Lord expresses a boldness that is captivating liken to the stories of Queen Esther and Deborah in the bible. Both were Godly women to admire whom I like to call "the beauty of brains."

ESTHER'S WISDOM

Esther's story begins with Queen Vashti, a very audacious and defiant woman of that particular time. Her husband King Xerxes made a request for her to come and stand before his council so they could see how beautiful she was, but she refused. Since he would never allow a woman to make a fool of him, he became very angry with her and as a result he began the search for a new queen. Mordecai, a member of King Xerxes court, brought his cousin Esther, a girl of Jewish descent, to the palace in hopes that she would have a chance at becoming queen. After viewing the runway show of potential candidates, Esther turned out to be a big hit. The King loved Esther more than the other young women and placed a crown upon her head appointing her as queen.

Like any story goes, things were going well at first but eventually they took a turn for the worse. Mordecai told Esther about a scheme two guards had devised to kill King Xerxes. Ether informed Xerxes, thus saving his life; giving Mordecai and herself a respectable relationship with the king. However a guy named Haman would soon ease his way in with impure motive.

Haman was given a high position in the king's court, which added to his already arrogant personality. With his position, Haman demanded that when he walked into the room, everyone bow down to him. Standing on his belief that he will only bow down to God, Mordecai did not grant Haman his request. Of course Haman didn't take Mordecai's response well; Haman plotted to kill all of the Jews, Esther and Mordecai's people.

Haman was able to persuade King Xerxes to kill the Jews. So, Mordecai had no choice but to run to Esther for help. Initially, Esther was afraid to get involved with the situation because she wasn't allowed to come to the king without his request. The penalty for doing so was death. However, after going back and forth about it, Esther gave a courageous response,

> *Go and gather together all the Jews of Susa and fast for me. Do not eat or drink for three days, night or day. My maids and I will do the same. And then, though it is against the law, I will go in to see the king. If I must die, I must die.*

Esther 4:16

After the fast, Esther prepared a banquet for the king and Haman. During the banquet Queen Esther disclosed Haman's evil scheme to kill her people. The result was that Esther saved her people from destruction.

You may think that Esther was chosen because she was the most appealing to king Xerxes. Viewing this story from a natural mind only, you'd be right. More profoundly, Esther was chosen by God to be Queen for a reason. God used Queen Esther to save her people. Now she could have sat back and enjoyed her royal status, concerning herself only with being ready for when the king would call her to his chamber. But she didn't do that. She realized that she was worth more than her physical beauty to God and to her people.

Esther portrayed a boldness that most women did not have during that time. Certainly, Esther's first thought could have been to think that she was not a leader. But she didn't because *she was*! She was valuable and she had a purpose. God appointed her to that position, because there's always a snake lurking that would love the opportunity to destroy His people. The Lord needs willing and courageous vessels He can use to accomplish His will here on earth.

Esther was a woman who showed compassion toward her people. She took a genuine concern for their well-being. She did not have to listen to Mordecai. After all, her life had changed. She was queen and she had her own life. She lived in a palace! However, she realized that she had to do something to save her people from destruction and she showed the greatest kind of love by laying her life on the line for her people.

Lastly, Esther showed great wisdom. She knew what to do to get the King's attention, even in that particular situation. Her people were in danger and she was under the impression that she couldn't get to the one person who could put a stop to it all, which was King Xerxes. So, she called a fast. This was a smart move to call a fast. A fast evens out your emotions. When you go without food or distractions (things that would normally consume a lot of your time) by fasting, your entire being is totally dependent on God. When you get in tune with God's voice and gain clarity about the things that concern you, you can hear God's voice more clearly. Removing the clutter from your life through fasting, also removes all of the noise so that you are more in tune with the Holy Spirit.

Esther not only led by example, but her leadership also caused God's people to be on one accord. When God's people are on one accord it releases the power of the Holy Spirit. That's when miracles, signs, and wonders take place. Esther knew what step to take next. What a smart young lady!

Since she already had built a positive relationship with the king she demonstrated her ability to exemplify boldness and revealed Haman's plans to kill the Jews. In response, Xerxes put an immediate stop to it.

There is so much stored up in you that has yet to be tapped into. Don't limit yourself on who you think you should be. Remember that what God says about you and what He has placed inside you is more important than anything; it speaks volumes. It certainly did in Esther's case. And then there was Deborah.

DEBORAH'S WISDOM

Now, the story of Deborah came a little bit before Esther. It begins with Moses and Joshua and transitions into how Deborah enters the story. Beginning in Exodus, the people of Israel were under oppression and in exile in Egypt so God raised up a man by the named of Moses to lead the people into the Promised Land. The Israelites' faith wasn't stable. By the time of Moses death they were only able to make it out of Egypt but not into the Promised Land. Before he died, Moses groomed Joshua to take over. Joshua lead the people and they entered into the promised land. But God didn't not allow Joshua to defeat all of Israel's enemies. He left some of Israel's enemies behind to see if Israel would be faithful to Him later on in the future. A couple generations after Joshua died the Israelites grew further away from God and started worshipping the Baals.

God allowed the Israelites enemies to conquer them and force them back into slavery. With no leader in place, God raised up "judges" to lead the people especially in the area of war. The role of a judge was to bring deliverance to God's people through battle by God's grace. In today's society a judge would be considered to be a leadership position just like a president or king but also judging cases like a judge in a court room. Additionally, the only time the Israelites were in right standing with God was when they had a judge to lead and assist in their freedom.

There were several judges that God called but many of them were not consistent in their faith and portrayed poor leadership; Samson & Gideon for example. However, a woman named Deborah rose above the inconsistency. Deborah was distinguished as the noblest of all the judges. She was not only the leader of the Israelites, she was a prophetess too. To be a prophet your heart and ear has to be very close to God in effort to deliver a timely message to God's people. Because the people were still defiant the Lord handed them over to Jabin, king of Canaan and his army commander Sisera. Being the heroine that she was, Deborah summoned Barak, the son of Abinoam of Naphtali, and challenged him because the Lord wanted him to lead the people in battle for freedom. Barak was afraid to go and would only go if Deborah went with him. So she went, but Barak lead the people in battle. However, because Barak was afraid and lacked faith she prophesied that the victory would go to a woman. As a result, the victory went to a woman named Jael, who lured Sisera into a tent by offering him food and then by striking him in his head.

The moral of this story is that Deborah was a phenomenal leader. She was an instrumental player in delivering her people from captivity. Another point to make is that she was a woman! We're talking Old Testament here. A woman in leadership was unheard of but God chose her to lead and he doesn't make mistakes during His selection process. He knows exactly what He's doing. He chose a woman who had exceptional characteristics. She was a warrior, agitator, prophetess, and ruler. To be this kind of woman, you can't focus on what society says you should be. You have to go with what God poured inside you. Then you must walk in boldness, faith, and *wisdom* to get the job done. That's what Deborah did. As a judge and warrior, she followed the leading of the Lord. She displayed great wisdom to know what do, when to do it, and how to do it.

APPLYING WISDOM TO EVERYDAY LIFE

As a follower of Christ and a woman of God, you should without a doubt desire wisdom. It's an attractive trait to have. Proverbs 31:10 says, "A capable, intelligent, *and* virtuous woman—who is he who can find her? She is far more precious than jewels *and* her value is far above rubies *or* pearls." Are you a woman of wisdom? Are you wise when it comes to the words that come out of your mouth? Do you apply wisdom in your interactions with others? Are you wise when choosing friends? Do you include God in your decision making or are you led by your emotions? Food for thought.

———————————

This week I challenge you to read a little of the book of Proverbs. In your prayers consider becoming more aware of the moments when it is necessary to apply wisdom to a current situation. At all times, seek God about everything you do and say and you'll always come out on top. Forget what the world tells you. Your brain makes you beautiful!

CHAPTER 5

LOVE GOD. LOVE PEOPLE. LOVE YOU.

"And you must love the LORD your God with all your heart, all your soul, all your mind, and all your strength. 'The second is equally important: 'Love your neighbor as yourself. No other commandment is greater than these."

Mark 12:30-31 (NLT)

What is love? In simplest terms, the answer is Jesus. Jesus displayed ultimate example when dying on the cross for our sins. The bible also gives us countless examples of Jesus' obedience to God, his service to others, his humility, and his nonjudgmental character.

Walking in our Christian identity means that we become more like Christ every day. We desire to please God with our life. We see the world like Christ sees it. We serve others like Christ served. We walk in a spirit of humility. We see the best in others when our natural reaction would be to see the worst in them. Jesus said the commandment to love is the greatest commandment of all (Mark 12:30-31).

If there were other commandments, but the commandment to love God and love people is the greatest commandment of all, what does that mean? How does that effect how we live our lives? Do we forget about the other commandments? Are they not important? Well, to answer these questions in a nutshell, it's important to understand what it means to love God as an act of obedience.

LOVE AS AN ACT OF OBEDIENCE

In John Chapter 14 Jesus shares with believers how to express their love, if they truly love him. This is by keeping his commandments (John 14:15). We know the two greatest commandments in the simplest terms is to "love God and love people." However, there are so many other commandments to abide by. Keeping up with a daily "what to do and not do list" outside of a normal day to day tasks would be quite daunting to say the least. However when I truly think about what Jesus was talking about in this scripture, I think about my submission to my husband. Now if you think I'm going off topic, just stay with me, we're going somewhere.

The book of Ephesians tells us about husbands and wives:

*Wives, submit to your own husbands, as to the Lord. For the husband is the head of the wife even as Christ is the head of the church, his body, and is himself its **Savior**. Now as the church submits to*

Christ, so also wives should submit in everything to their husbands.

Ephesians 5:22-24

According to the Word of God, wives are supposed to submit to their husbands even though for some ladies, the word submission in this passage makes them cringe. Even though this passage is not solely about marriage, it's important to understand there is a deeper meaning here.

In the same way, when we love our husbands, even though we may not get it right every time, we're intentional about doing what's best for them by placing them before ourselves. We spend quality time, prepare dinner, do laundry, and clean our home. Anything to serve them and place them at the forefront. In the same way, loving Christ means we also spend time with him through prayer and fasting, studying the Word, loving others, and being the best Christian example we could possibly be. When we do these things we're not only showing God we love him but we are also demonstrating obedience. So we have to really ask ourselves some questions. Do I truly love Christ? Do I make time for him daily? Am I willing to put my desires aside to go seek his face? Do I put anything else before him?

I once heard someone say that she's not a morning person and she never has been. She said for years she struggled with getting up in the morning to have quiet time with the Lord. She would get on track and do well for some months and then fall off. Then she would do well for a few weeks until she failed again. Eventually, she became purposeful about becoming a morning person so that she could be intentional about Christ. In every relationship we have to want someone that's going to be intentional about loving us and spending time with us. Being intentional is important in our relationships with our friends and our family. If we don't make time for one another our relationships will fail. I know I would question if a person truly cared about me if they stopped putting the time in to simply call or hang out from time to time.

If there is any area in your life where you feel that you could be more intentional about your relationship with Christ I encourage you to make those changes. Even if it's baby steps, any step is better than no step. Show Christ your love today.

LOVE AS AN ACT OF SERVICE

Another way to show love is through acts of service. This life is not about you. Let me say it again. Although God has given you life, it's not about you. Not at all. It's about God and about people. There's that phrase again! You're here to show Christ to a dying world. One of the ways you can do that is by serving. Now of course you can serve in your church by joining a ministry! Currently I serve as a Sunday school teacher. I develop creative lesson plans to get girls excited about Jesus.

You can also pay it forward by buying someone's groceries or paying for the person behind you in the drive-thru. If you have a team of people you lead, it never hurts to get in the trenches with them and help them out from time to time. When they see that you're willing to work alongside them they'll like you better for it. If you're just an employee the same goes for you! If you see a colleague in need, go ask her if she needs some help. What I've found to be true is that when you help people on the job you reap what you sow. Many times you'll find that people will want to get projects completed for you a lot faster than they would for someone else. If you need something they have no problem with helping you because you've made yourself available to them when you did not have to.

You can also treat a homeless person to their next meal or offer them the cash to purchase what they want. You can be intentional about serving at a homeless shelter or a food pantry. There are so many ways that you can serve, but ultimately serving can be an open door for you to tell someone about the goodness of Jesus. You also don't know what a person may need so remember to:

Let love be genuine. Abhor what is evil; hold fast to what is good. Love one another with brotherly affection. Outdo one another in showing honor. Do not be slothful in zeal, be fervent in spirit, serve the Lord. Rejoice in hope, be patient in tribulation, be constant in prayer. Contribute to the needs of the saints and seek to show hospitality.

Romans 12:9-13

The more you show love to others especially women, the more people will want to be around you. There are women that are just plain nice ladies, and those are the type of women I want in my circle! While society may tell us that women love to argue, compete, and talk trash about one another, I truly believe women are yearning to connect with one another. I truly believe that women want to have other women they can trust. We need women in our lives to lift us up. We need those ladies that are willing to go to war in the spirit realm for us when we're at our lowest point. We need a sister in Christ that can *understand exactly where we're coming from* when we're having a bad day and not judge us for it. That's service. Praying for someone *besides yourself* is an act of service to them. Try it some time. This may be the easiest most powerful act of service ever. Simply ask, "My sister, how can I be praying for you today?"

LOVE AS AN ACT OF HUMILITY

I love listening to sermons online especially at work. It helps me get through the mundane tasks of my job a lot faster and I get nourishment at the same time. Not too long ago one of my favorite preachers said something that was quite simple and yet so profound. He said, when you talk about the character of another person as Christians we should *present them on their best day*. As he went on to speak he mentioned that sometimes people have negative moments. Even though someone has upset you or you're often disappointed with the actions or even words of another person none of that matters. What matters is that you present them on their best day.

What does it mean to present someone on their best day? Well, that means with all the time that you've known a person you find the day that you enjoyed them the most and those are the characteristics you share. You don't bad mouth them to others and communicate what a horrible person they are. You have to do what is right and see them the way God sees them. I think this is certainly helpful for those who may be known to gossip. Some of us can chew a person up and spit them out. However, the sad part is that we are all sinners. So we aren't perfect either. I'm a lot better in this area than I used to be, especially concerning those that have wronged me, but I still need to work on it.

It is important to remain humble because humility allows us to show the love of God. Remaining humble causes you to present yourself in a manner that doesn't come off as judgmental or as if you are better than they anyone else. Demonstrating humility also puts you in a position of being approachable and relatable; two necessary attributes to have when you want to share the love of Jesus or simply *"represent"* *Him.*

Humility is love at its best because Jesus walked in humility no matter how awesome and gifted he was. A boastful person walks around with an attitude that places other beneath themselves and raises them up. That isn't love. The bible tells us that love is not boastful (1 Corinthians 13:4).

A woman that walks with poise, grace, and class always has a kind word to say. She is loving and doesn't consider herself to be better than anyone else. There are several times in the bible where Jesus represents the best response. Liken to the story of the adulterous women. Society sought to tear her down, but Jesus has always advised people not to judge.

> *"Teacher," they said to Jesus, "this woman was caught in the act of adultery. The law of Moses says to stone her. What do you say?" They were trying to trap him into saying something they could use against him, but Jesus stooped down and wrote in the dust with his finger. They kept demanding an answer, so he stood up again and said, "All right, but let the one who has never sinned throw the first stone!" Then he stooped down again and wrote in the dust. When the accusers heard this, they slipped away one by one, beginning with the oldest, until only Jesus was left in the middle of the crowd with the woman. Then Jesus stood up again and said to the woman, "Where are your accusers? Didn't even one of them condemn you?" "No, Lord," she said. And Jesus said, "Neither do I. Go and sin no more."*

John 8:4-11

The community of the adulterous woman wanted to convict her of her offense. While everyone else was looking down on her, Jesus the ultimate authority, did not. Instead he loved her. So if Jesus didn't tell her how awful she is what right do we have doing this to others? Now, I'm not saying that purposely living immorally is acceptable because it is not. We are called to a higher standard. What I am saying is that at the moment Jesus said, "Go and sin no more," she was no longer the same woman. She was freed from her sin. She was a new woman with a new identity in Christ. No matter what identity a woman wears, slander is never going to help her with her identity crisis. Love your sisters in Christ. Present them on their best day. Stay humble.

LOVE AS AN ACT OF GRACE

Mentioning love without mentioning grace and mercy is impossible. There is God's grace toward us, but also our grace toward others. As the singer/song writer Warren Barfield said "grace I receive so grace I must give." I think one of the best examples of grace and mercy is one of Jesus last words on the cross, "Father forgive them, for they know not what they do (Luke 23:24)." After every horrific thing that was done to Jesus, from the persecution to the beating he endured, he still asked our Father in heaven to forgive his enemies. If Jesus could forgive those that hurt him, certainly with time we could forgive those that hurt us.

What about the prodigal son? The story of the prodigal son is about a young man of a rich father who decided to run off with his inheritance. His father allowed him to go, but at some point after the son lost everything and found himself living amongst pigs, he realized that the abundant life he had with his father was truly living. He decided to go back home hoping his father would accept him back. Here's what happened:

"I will arise and go to my father, and I will say to him, "Father, I have sinned against heaven and before you. I am no longer worthy to be called your son. Treat me as one of your hired servants."' And he arose and came to his father. But while he was still a long way off, his father saw him and felt compassion, and ran and embraced him and kissed him. And the son said to him, 'Father, I have sinned against heaven and before you. I am no longer worthy to be called your son. 'But the father said to his servants, 'Bring quickly the best robe, and put it on him, and put a ring on his hand, and shoes on his feet. And bring the fattened calf and kill it, and let us eat and celebrate. For this my son was dead, and is alive again; he was lost, and is found.' And they began to celebrate."

Luke 15:18-24

The story of the prodigal son is a story that lets us know that even if we run away from God, He still loves us and he's waiting for us to return to Him. Most would think that after the father's son ran off with his inheritance, the father would be done with him. That was not the case in this story. His father showed grace and mercy toward him by not treating him harshly but instead by showing him a kind of favor that could not be earned by works but only through unconditional love. Not only did the father run toward his son as he saw him in the distance, he placed a big ring on his finger, gave him a brand new wardrobe, and threw him the biggest party! That's how much he loved his son, and this story is a mirror image of God's love for us. Not only did the father forgive his son, he also restored everything that he had lost while he was away. Again, if God can forgive us and restore us, then we can forgive ourselves and forgive others as well.

And finally there was Peter. Peter was a disciple known as "the rock." Jesus named Peter "the rock" because he recognized Jesus as the Messiah (Matthew 16:18). Jesus response was to build his church on the rock. Peter had a key role in building the church and advancing the kingdom of God here on earth. Although Peter was supposed to be an integral player on "team Jesus" Peter had some bad plays:

> *When they had finished breakfast, Jesus said to Simon Peter, "Simon, son of John, do you love me more than these?" He said to him, "Yes, Lord; you know that I love you." He said to him, "Feed my lambs." He said to him a second time, "Simon, son of John, do you love me?" He said to him, "Yes, Lord; you know that I love you." He said to him, "Tend my sheep." He said to him the third time, "Simon, son of John, do you love me?" Peter was grieved because he said to him the third time, "Do you love me?" and he said to him, "Lord, you know*

everything; you know that I love you." Jesus

said to him, "Feed my sheep." Truly, truly, I

say to you, when you were young, you used to

dress yourself and walk wherever you wanted,

but when you are old, you will stretch out your

hands, and another will dress you and carry

you where you do not want to go." (This he

said to show by what kind of death he was to

glorify God.) And after saying this he said to

him, "Follow me."

John 21:15-19

Here we are sometime later in scripture and we witness Jesus and Peter having a tough conversation. What made Jesus question Peter's love for him? After all Peter was "the rock." Peter was one of the sole contributors to the early church but here we see Jesus continually questioning his love and commitment. Well, although Jesus placed a lot of responsibility on Peter, Peter wasn't always committed to Christ. In this passage we see that Jesus asked Peter three times if he loved him. Many say that those three times represents the three times that Peter eventually denied Jesus. Thank God for His grace!

How would you feel if a family member, friend, boyfriend, or spouse denied knowing who you were publicly? That's betrayal. Guess what? Peter betrayed Jesus three times. Although Peter sinned against Jesus in such a hurtful and possibly humiliating way, Jesus still forgave him. Peter didn't completely understand right away that Jesus' constant questioning was related to unconditional love and not the fickle love that he had been presenting Christ. This was Peter's moment to learn that Christ would not accept a partial commitment. Christ had plans for Peter, therefore more was going to be required of him. Jesus was requiring unconditional love.

The story of Peter is a story about restoration. Although Peter denied Christ three times, by understanding the need to show unconditional love to Christ especially through obedience, Peter was restored to rightful standing and was charged to lead Jesus' followers. Several times in the bible we find these stories of God restoring people to right standing when they turn their hearts back to Him. So not only was Peter forgiven, but he got a promotion to lead the people and start the early church after Christ's death. That's grace!

I love this story because it shows us that no matter how many times we walk away from Christ, he's waiting for us with open arms to come back home. He's willing to restore us and have mercy on us even though we don't deserve it. He has plans to prosper us and to give us a great future (Jeremiah 29:11).

The problem that we sometimes have is that after Christ forgives us we need to let go and forgive ourselves. We can hinder the plans that God has for us if we're still harboring over the things we did in the past. It can get really bad when we focus on how much we mess up in a day! If you wrote down how many times you did something wrong in a day, you'd be pretty down on yourself. If you count how many times you had a bad attitude, forgot to pray and read your bible the number could be really high. Be kind to yourself.

In regards to Peter, he made major contributions toward the spreading of the gospel. But what if Peter focused on his shortcomings instead of Christ's forgiveness and restoration? Where would the church be today? As God shows grace to you, you have to show grace to yourself.

This week find ways to demonstrate the love of Christ by saying a kind word,, offering an act of service, or showing grace. And don't forget to be loving to yourself. Being loving to those around you lets them know how much Christ's loves them. Share the love!

CHAPTER 6

WOMAN ON A MISSION

Go therefore and make disciples of all nations.

(Matthew 28:19-20)

If you research the word "disciple" you'll learn that the word means: a student. Matthew 10:24 says, "A disciple is not above his teacher, nor a servant above his master." Therefore, the disciples were students and their teacher was Jesus. In the New Testament we find several stories of Jesus teaching the disciples. They may not have realized it right away, but Jesus wasn't merely teaching them for the sake of teaching them. After Jesus' resurrection, he left the disciples with a job to do. He says:

"All authority in heaven and on earth has been given to me. Go therefore and make disciples of all nations, baptizing them in the name of the Father and of the Son and of the Holy Spirit, teaching them to observe all that I have commanded you. And behold, I am with you always, to the end of the age."

Matthew 28:18-20

In the same way that Jesus left the disciples with a job to do, he has instructed us to follow suit. We are Christ's modern day disciples. We are his students. We are his followers. We are not called to sit back and look pretty, ladies. Although we are all beautiful, we are called to so much more, and it is time we get moving!

God wants to see his name made great here on earth! Scripture says to "go make disciples" (Matthew 28:19). Which means that the movement Jesus started doesn't stop. It continues! We have to go tell others about Jesus.

PURPOSEFUL INTEGRITY

When considering evangelism (telling others about Jesus) it's important to be strategic in how you share the gospel. One of the loudest and most productive ways to share Christ with others is simply by how you live your life every day. One of the ways that I've learned to represent Christ at work is by having integrity. Most people already know that "I profess" to be a Christ follower, but in today's society, sometimes words doesn't mean much. In some parts of America, everybody claims Jesus but they don't live out this walk on a daily basis. No matter where I am, I try to make sure I have integrity. So what does it mean to have integrity?

When you're purposeful about walking with integrity it means that you are intentional about everything you do. If you set a deadline, you try your best to meet it. You stand by your word. It also means that you live by honesty. If you made a mistake you own up to it. It doesn't matter if someone makes fun of you for it. Nevertheless, it's the right thing to do. The bible says, "Having a good conscience, so that, when you are slandered, those who revile your good behavior in Christ may be put to shame (1 Peter 3:16)."

However, more often than not, people will have more respect for you, when you own up to your mistakes. It also means that you stay out of trouble. In his letter to Titus, Paul says, "Show yourself in all respects to be a model of good works, and in your teaching show integrity, dignity, and sound speech that cannot be condemned, so that an opponent may be put to shame, having nothing evil to say about us (Titus 2:7-8)." When others are causing problems (or even demonstrating a false identity in Christ), you make sure that you are nowhere near the problem. Additionally, you should make sure you are not the problem! At the end of the day, all you have is your name and your faith! As a woman on a mission, you should never want to discredit your name or the name of Christ. You should make every attempt to make sure your name and Christ's name are in good standing. Your integrity means everything!

As the years go by, one of the things I've noticed is that whether you know it or not, people are always watching you. The way you live your life speaks volumes. As Christians we should "aim at what is honorable not only in the Lord's sight but also in the sight of man (2 Corinthians 8:21)." You can lead others to Christ or persuade people to dislike everything they believe is true about Christ, by your lifestyle. There may be times that verbally telling others about Christ may not be the most strategic move, especially in the workplace, but people will see the way you live your life and they will know something is different about you.

You also want to make sure that you are consistent with the way you live. It's not helpful to live with integrity one day and then be caught in a deceitful act the next day. Your message needs to be firm and consistent. If it's not consistent, then you can end up confusing those around you and that's not helpful to Christ's cause. The bible says, "Therefore, my beloved brothers, be steadfast, immovable, always abounding in the work of the Lord, knowing that in the Lord your labor is not in vain (1 Corinthians 15:58)." This doesn't mean that we have to be perfect every single day. We certainly will have some "off" days. However, it does mean that we start each morning asking for God's help as we endeavor to live our life for God out loud to make more disciples.

This is the kind of Christianity the world needs to see. Instead of a society of lukewarm, inconsistent people claiming they know Christ, how about together we strive to become a society of people, a society of royal women that are purposeful every time they get up in the morning. Women who are focused as the day gets started; before the meetings and the grocery shopping, and the laundry etc. All of these things are important, but how about together, being deliberate in making sure we are representing Christ in everything we do, that we say, and in how we live. What if together, as royal women we make Christ our "to-do" list? If we keep Christ at the forefront of each day then maybe we can resemble the body that God desires and inspire others to try Jesus. Let your light shine (Matthew 5:16)!

SHARING IS CARING

Think about all the people you come in contact with every day. You can always be willing to say, "God bless you" as you receive your receipt at the grocery store. I know when someone says it to me, I quickly make sure I say it back! You can call up a friend or family member and ask how you could be praying for them that week. One of the things I like to do is text a young lady and let her know that God thinks she's beautiful. There are so many ways you can share the goodness of Jesus with others. It doesn't take much.

In today's society social media is one of the main ways we communicate to large numbers of people. What you say and post on the internet can be a huge encouragement to the body of believers and unbelievers alike or it can hinder your witness. It doesn't mean that you have to clog up everyone's newsfeed with Jesus posts, but it does mean that what you say matters. People are glued to the internet these days. The new normal is to check your phone all day long. Some ladies make posts to complain about somebody or something that just happened. Maybe you've seen it. Everyone knows at least one person that likes to "go off" on social media. Social media can be a great tool to let the world know about the love of Christ. I'll be honest, sometimes people think it's a cliché to be the "Jesus freak" especially when it comes to social media. I will admit I was once that person that wanted "to be normal." I wanted to fit in especially since everyone thought all I talked about was Jesus. Now I realize that I was born to stand out and I don't care what anyone says about me:

> *I have told the glad news of deliverance in the great congregation; behold, I have not restrained my lips, as you know, O Lord. I have not hidden your deliverance within my heart; I have spoken of your faithfulness and your salvation; I have not concealed your steadfast love and your faithfulness from the great congregation.*
>
> Psalm 40:9-10

Rejoice about the goodness of God and be glad to share the great things he's done! When you look back over your life and think about all the great things God has done you should be so excited to tell others about the amazing God you serve. So post a picture of your devotional. Share an uplifting scripture with others. Write the blog that you always wanted to write. Write the book you always wanted to write. Develop the

Christian magazine you've been putting off for years. Don't be afraid to be who you are.

Speaking of telling others the good news of Jesus Christ, I have to tell you about my Father-in-law. He's one of the boldest men I know. When you ask him how he's doing he says, *"I'm blessed, wise, in good health, and debt free every day, because Jesus Christ is the head of my life!"* I usually laugh because I don't know anyone that responds that same way every time. It's also a *very long* response. However, there are two things you can take from his response. The first being that this response is his confession. He quotes and meditates on 3 John 1:2. He believes the words that he speaks and as Christians we know the words we speak have power. The second is that his response is his witness. He's gives this response to everyone. He shows no partiality to whom he offers his confession. The bible says, "so faith comes by hearing and hearing the word of Christ (Romans 10:17)." The more he shares his response the more his faith builds and the more he's building the faith of others.

Whether someone hears the word of God during a church service or simply by having a conversation with my father-in-law, people need to hear the word. It's up to us to share it!

THE INVITATION

Maybe communication isn't your strong suit, but you still want to help. One of the most impactful ways you can share Christ with others is by inviting them to fellowship with you. You can invite someone to church, to a small group, or even your young adult ministry game night! God wants us to bring others to Christ and he also desires fellowship amongst believers.

> "We proclaim to you what we have seen and
> heard, so that you also may have fellowship
> with us. And our fellowship is with the Father
> and with his Son, Jesus Christ."
>
> 1 John 1: 1-3

This passage stresses the importance of not only proclaiming the good news of Jesus Christ but also speaks to the connection of winning souls so that those who choose to believe can fellowship with Christ and be in community with other believers. The author John is emphasizing how much he wants nonbelievers to enjoy the life that Christ has to offer. You may not realize it, but there are so many people in this world who have never stepped foot inside a church before. We have to be careful when making assumptions that all people have a good understanding of the Christian faith.

Now before you make the invitation, the first thing you want to do is develop the relationship. It'll be pretty difficult to persuade someone to attend an event that they don't identify with, especially if they are not invested in their relationship with you. That means if you don't know the person that well you're going to need to put in some effort into getting to know them.

So what will your invitation be? Maybe you can start a book club with a group of ladies or invite a co-worker to see your favorite Christian band in concert. You could also invite a young lady to the next women's day event at your church. Additionally, there is always fun ideas like coffee or shopping trips! You can choose several ways to invite someone to Christ, but most of all make sure the invitation is loving and kind.

———————

This week as you prepare to think about all the things you have planned to do, make sure to add "tell somebody about Jesus." Remember, whether it's verbal or non-verbal communication, the choices you make speak volumes. Choose to be purposeful about advancing God's kingdom. Let your light shine!

CHAPTER 7

YOUR HEARTS DESIRE

Delight yourself in the LORD,

and he will give you the desires of your heart

Psalm 37:4 ESV

We're at the last chapter and we've learned about so many different concepts and people in the bible. It may have been a lot to take in. You may even be overwhelmed with trying to walk in your new identity. Remember, grace! Whenever you feel overwhelmed or like you have to be perfect to please God, just shout, "grace!" We are God's precious possession and He thought you and I were worth dying for! Do you accept that truth? *You and I are to die for!* Some years ago, people would use the phrase "to die for" when they would talk about something they loved or really enjoyed like a new restaurant or a new outfit. But I think it can be used again when talking about how much Christ loves us. He accepted us in our sin so that we don't have to be perfect. You and I are worth that much my friend.

All God wants you to do is to continue striving to walk in his reflection and represent him wherever you go. Don't worry about messing up sometimes. God wants you to be intentional about your love for him and your love for others. He wants you to brag on his love and how good he is to you. If you can do that, he promised in his word that he will give you the desires of your heart (Psalm 37:4).

REWARDS ON EARTH

This is certainly great news because walking in your new threads won't always be easy, but there is a reward that is waiting to you, if you remain faithful.

"The rules of the Lord are true, and righteous

altogether. More to be desired are they than

gold, even much fine gold; sweeter also than

honey and drippings of the honeycomb.

Moreover, by them is your servant warned; in

keeping them there is great reward."

Psalm 19:9-11

We also have to realize that when we look at how others are living, we have no idea if they are truly fulfilled. One of the blessings that comes from a true relationship with Christ is that your security, joy, and fulfillment comes from Christ. Therefore, as he gives you the desires of your heart, your desires will reflect his desires for you. Romantic relationships, clothes, or professional success won't move you. Whatever, represents Christ and whatever pleases Christ will please you. It's what you'll crave!

"As the deer longs for streams of water, so I

long for you, O God. I thirst for God, the

living God. When can I go and stand before

him?"

Psalm 42 1-2

Not only will God shape your desires, He will give you your heart's desire if you don't quit. So what are those things you have laid up before the Lord? What is it that you need? What is it that you desire? As the apple of God's eye (Psalm 17:8) He wants you to be well. He wants you to prosper! He wants you to succeed! He wants the very best for his daughter. He will give you good health. He will give you a peace you could never imagine. God wants these things for you because he loves you.

REWARDS IN HEAVEN

Not only does God want to bless you while you're here on Earth, he wants to give you the ultimate reward, heaven. That's the end goal; heaven.

Paul who was mentioned earlier, realized the goal. He talked about the goal often.

> *Not that I have already obtained this or am already perfect, but I press on to make it my own, because Christ Jesus has made me his own. Brothers, I do not consider that I have made it my own. But one thing I do: forgetting what lies behind and straining forward to what lies ahead, I press on toward the goal for the prize of the upward call of God in Christ Jesus. Let those of us who are mature think this way, and if in anything you think otherwise, God will reveal that also to you. Only let us hold true to what we have attained.*
>
> *Brothers, join in imitating me, and keep your eyes on those who walk according to the example you have in us. For many, of whom I have often told you and now tell you even with tears, walk as enemies of the cross of Christ. Their end is destruction, their god is their*

belly, and they glory in their shame, with

minds set on earthly things. But our

citizenship is in heaven, and from it we await a

Savior, the Lord Jesus Christ, who will

transform our lowly body to be like his glorious

body, by the power that enables him even to

subject all things to himself.

Philippians 3:12-21

This world is not our home. Like Paul said, our citizenship is in heaven and we must remember that. We also have to keep that in the forefront of our minds. Even as I think about relationships that I build with others, organizations that I may join, and career options that I think through, I always have to consider whether or not my choices please God, because my ultimate goal is heaven. That's where I want to be when it's all said and done. There is a reward in heaven greater than anything we could ever expect here on earth if we stay on track. God has prepared this reward just for you; his daughter, in mind when he prepared it.

> *"Let not your hearts be troubled. Believe in*
> *God; believe also in me. In my Father's house*
> *are many rooms ("mansions" -KJV). If it were*
> *not so, would I have told you that I go to*
> *prepare a place for you? And if I go and prepare*
> *a place for you, I will come again and will take*
> *you to myself, that where I am you may be also.*
> *And you know the way to where I am going."*
> *Thomas said to him, "Lord, we do not know*
> *where you are going. How can we know the*
> *way?" Jesus said to him, "I am the way, and*
> *the truth, and the life. No one comes to the*
> *Father except through me.*

John 14 1-6 ESV

God loves you so much and he wants you all to himself. This passage lets you know that he has you in mind. When he brings you home to himself you'll never have to worry ever again. You'll never have to be concerned about food, shelter, pay checks, school, or if a guy is interested or disinterested in you! You'll never have to worry about your job, the next step in your career, sickness or disease (Revelation 21:4). What's more is that he has a mansion with many rooms prepared just for you my dear queen! This is what we are striving for. With Christ, we truly live.

I want to leave you with Paul's word to his younger brother in Christ, Timothy. It's so interesting how the word of God is a timeless book, an instructional manual, and so powerful. These words that Paul writes incredibly reflect today's society. He says,

> *"I charge you in the presence of God and of*
> *Christ Jesus, who is to judge the living and the*
> *dead, and by his appearing and his kingdom:*

preach the word; be ready in season and out of season; reprove, rebuke, and exhort, with complete patience and teaching. For the time is coming when people will not endure sound teaching, but having itching ears they will accumulate for themselves teachers to suit their own passions, and will turn away from listening to the truth and wander off into myths. **As for you, always be sober-minded, endure suffering, do the work of an evangelist, fulfill your ministry.**

For I am already being poured out as a drink offering, and the time of my departure has come. I have fought the good fight, I have finished the race, and I have kept the faith. Henceforth there is laid up for me the crown of righteousness, which the Lord, the righteous judge, will award to me on that Day, and not only to me but also to all who have loved his appearing.

2 Timothy 4:1-8

Paul's instructions command us all to continue fighting the fight and running the race. No matter what state the world is in today, we can't give up. Our job is to do the work of an evangelist. In whatever way possible we must reflect Christ. Years, ago one of my favorite songs was called "Reflect You" by Warren Barfield. I always loved the line "you are the sun, I am the moon, I reflect you." That's what we must do! That is our ministry. If we stay committed there is the most beautiful crown in store for us ladies! The crown of righteousness! It's worth more than any other crown worn by any other queen in time or space and it's better than any crown you'd ever receive at a pageant. This is what it's all about. It's time to get to work.

Accepting your new identity will not be an easy task. Like anything else in life you have to take it day by day. If you're up for the challenge, I dare you to be consistent in wearing your new identity as God's masterpiece. It's may take some getting used to, but you'll soon see that life will never be the same. It will change for the better. You may run into some tough days, but you'll have the tools necessary to overcome. As you're moving forward, keep this guidebook along with your bible close by to refer to and as a reminder of who you are and whose you are. You are a daughter of the King and you are priceless!

I ended my relationship with John for the final time at the age of 23. It was the first time in my life that I felt like I could breathe. Prior to that time, I would wake up night after night in a cold sweat feeling restless because I had not accepted my value. I wrote this book because I don't want that for you. I certainly don't want you to continue down that road for as many years as I did. Most importantly God doesn't want that for you. Once I moved on, I had an exercise that I would do to stay focused. I would write out goals for each season of the year on post-it notes and stick them to my wall. Each time that I met a goal I would cross it off the list. These goals would consist of professional and spiritual goals. Sometimes in a season I would not meet a goal, so I would write it down for the next season. On smaller post-it notes I would write down things I wanted to remember about myself and I would look at these notes daily. My post-it notes would have words like: poise, grace, confidence, intelligence, wisdom etc. The more that I looked at these words on my wall the more I began to emulate what these words meant and people noticed. This week try to write out words that represent you as God's masterpiece and stick them to your wall. Overtime as you begin to take on your new identity take notice of how your identity begins to change. Get excited! You're on your way!

Closing Prayer

Let today be the day you make your commitment toward becoming and embracing yourself as God's masterpiece. It is my hope that you never look back. If you're ready, let's stand together and agree in prayer.

God I pray that you help every woman that reads this book. Wipe all her tears away. Let her know that you love her. Let her know that you've provided a way out. Let her know that you've planned a life for her that's greater than she's planned for herself and greater than what's she's limited herself to. Let her know that today can be the best day of her life if she chooses you and the life you've planned for her. I pray that she will become confident and walk in poise and grace knowing that she is beautiful and intelligent with so many characteristics that she has yet to tap into. I pray that she comes to that realization now and that she realizes her value is so high that she will begin to walk with a glow. And as she walks with a glow people will begin to notice the Jesus inside of her because of how radiant she is. I also pray that you will also begin to reveal to her, her purpose in life along with the gifts and talents that you've hidden inside her. I pray that you will open a whole new world to her and that she won't allow individuals in her life that will hold her back, put her down, or cage her in but that she will attract people with a similar identity that will encourage her, pray for her, and value her allowing her to walk in freedom and to be the woman you have designed for her to be. I pray that she will realize that she is in charge of her own happiness and that she is beautiful from the inside out. She does not need to compare herself to society's standards. This will be the best day of her life! Even as the days move forward and she has tough days she will rely on you. She will give her burdens to you and she will overcome. Nothing will be too hard because you are with her. There are so many great days in store for her! Finally, I pray that she will place the crown upon her head and walk out of darkness into your marvelous light never to look back again!

Amen.